The Floating Door

M. E. Silverman

Glass Lyre Press

Copyright © 2018 M.E. Silverman

Paperback ISBN: 978-1-941783-46-7

All rights reserved: except for the purpose of quoting brief passages for review, no part of this book may be reproduced or transmitted in any form or by any means, electronic or mechanical, including photocopying, recording, or by any information storage and retrieval system, without permission in writing from the publisher.

Cover art: Tommy Ingberg
Author photo: Karen Sneddon
Design & layout: Steven Asmussen
Copyediting: Linda E. Kim

Glass Lyre Press, LLC
P.O. Box 2693
Glenview, IL 60025
www.GlassLyrePress.com

This book is dedicated to the best poem I ever wrote, born in 2006. We named her Isabel. In the Jewish tradition of blessing one's child: *May you be like Sarah, Rebecca, Rachel, and Leah. May God bless you and guard you. May God show you favor and be gracious to you. May God show you kindness and grant you peace.*

Grateful acknowledgment is made to the hard-working editors & staff of the following publications where these poems first appeared (some in slightly different forms):

A Cappella Zoo
Because I Said So: Anthology
Bloomsbury Anthology of Contemporary Jewish Poetry
Blue Monday Review
Crab Orchard Review
December
[Ex]tinguished and [Ex]tinct: An Anthology of Things that no Longer Exist
Festival Writer
Gingko Tree Review
Harstkill Review
The Labletter
The Liberal Media Made Me Do It: Poems Based on NPR & PBS
Mizmor L'David Anthology: The Shoah
Naugatuck River Review
North Chicago Review
Off The Coast
Prime Number Magazine
Provo Canyon
Red Earth Review
Scissors & Spackle
Tapestry
The Southern Poetry Anthology: Georgia
Tulane Review
Tupelo Quarterly
Veils, Halos and Shackles: International Poetry on the Abuse and Oppression of Women
Vision/Verse
Weave Magazine

Some poems appear in the chapbook *The Breath Before Birds Fly.*

Contents

I

Cupcakes	3
Tips	5
Noah Knocks on the Door, Drunk	6
Hurricane Dreams	7
Response to: Step on a Crack	8
Cokelore	9
Fumes	10
Response to: Don't Swallow your Gum or It will Grow into a Tree	11
Response to: Chocolate Causes Massive Acne	12
Mud Man	13
Miracle	14
Miracle Shoes	15
Sitting in a Simulated Space at the Atlantic Station IKEA in Atlanta, Georgia	16
Response to: You're Going to Dig a Hole to China	18
"I Don't Believe," She Said, "In You."	19
Response to: It's Getting Harder & Harder to Leave the House	20
Bait & Trap	21
Response to: Why Don't You Just Get Outta Here	22
Response to: I Can't Get Off the Couch	23
Returning to the Abortion Clinic	24
Menorah-Mama at Mt. Sinai	25
Dear Sister Dreydel,	27
Final Exam	30
Endings	31
Meditation before Falling Asleep	32
Finding my Father's Kinnor	33
Finding the Perfect Tune for the Last	34
Friday at Publix in Atlanta	36

II

Love Poem for Wings	41
Mud Angel	42
Undone	43
The Mermaid Meets Mud Angel	44
Sea Watching	49
Secret Wings	50
The Patience Stone at the Mobile Mini Children's Circus in Kabul	52
Spaces	53
Imaginary Prop List for an Abandoned Temple	55
On the Sixth Day	56
The Last Jew	57
Love Poem for Land Lines	59
The Last Jew's Wife	60
The Last Days of the Balkh Bastan (2013)	61
Yellow	63
Imaginary Stage for an Abandoned Temple	64
The Last Synagogue	65
The Last Jew Celebrates the New Year with his Dead Friend, Ishaq Levin	66
Interview with Z. S.	69
Finding Yehud	70
The Last Act of an Unwritten Play	75
Interview with Grandmother	76
Sometime after This	77
Glossary	79
About the Author	83

I

"God, how American to hope
they'll come to love their lives somehow, American
to say what is and isn't possible."

—Deborah Digges

Cupcakes

We watch her wet the little rings of hair
that fall over her ears with two globs of spit.
She utters the word *business*

& to the furl of her tongue,
a power rises, an energetic dance.
Our envious stomachs twitch.

We wait for the hours smoking stolen cigs
in front of Estelle's Old Time Motel,
freedom from mama to do what we want.

We know it's time to go
when she rubs burnt matches
over her almond eyes.

Gray geese flock above us,
fly out of their V-formation,
their soft sounds like sex

heard through a closed door.
We play ghosts-in-the-graveyard,
tell girl-secrets to Kitty, who spends

summers here in Mama's motel.
Three suits pass by
as silent as arousal. A boy

whose name begins with *No*
sits in an old Corvette drinking
chocolate milk. He eats Hostess cupcakes,

holds candy cigarettes & pretends he owns
the place. We want to trade,
to go into the rich A/C,

to take his treats, to poke
the proud rolls of his stomach
until he vomits brown.

My sister approaches
through the heat.
She asks for the last cake.

The boy tells her *no!*,
no! she can't come in, *no!*
she can't have this cake!

She whispers into the open window's crack.
I hear the slip of the car door's lock.
She slides inside.

Tips

Father loves *matzah* balls more than me,
more than anyone. He doesn't pause for them
to cool, a child with his prize.

I wait for the four glasses of wine,
the bitter herbs, the tightening
of his eyes & cheeks,

his shoulders & arms,
as he tells the same stories
every year: how he sacrificed

so much to be a Dad
after his own deserted them
with the rabbi's most buxom daughter,

how he spent his monthly ten-cent treat
on sci-fi books, the buses it took to get
out of Sheepshead Bay,

how his mother threw away issue one
of Action, now worth a quarter of a million,
because he once asked where his Dad had gone,

how he shouted out the open door
about her refusal to learn to drive,
to move from the tired bricks of Brooklyn,

to breach her routine that lasted for forty years,
the hot months he peddled down Fifth like a commandment
& up First delivering silk for tips.

So I stay seated. I
look at my hands
in my lap. We say the final *diaynu*.

Noah Knocks on the Door, Drunk

Open the door, dove.

Pull back the shade, son.

Let me & the gin—damnit!

      Between the ocean & rain, a boat.

      Between a boat & the sun, more rain.

      Between rain & a sky, stars, one sun.

I have a son, a father.

I have no son & one father.

I have no son, no father.

      Lord, let me not be the bird

who flies free who flies far

only to return, one olive leaf

in my mouth.

Hurricane Dreams

Because I always wanted one, my father has pulled a hairless cat out of my chest. He tells me about Abraham in Hebrew the way his father taught him.

I stare at the door in his lips. My ears are full of winter. I try to hear, I really do. Water presses against my body, pushes salty grime inside my mouth, my nose, every pore. It swallows the sun. Darkness soaks through me, makes me heavy & sleepy. He lifts me from the water, whispers words from the only stories he knows, says God calls Abraham to the land, gives them a child late in life, calls them chosen. A part of me knows my father is not God & cannot breathe life into something so small as me, curled like the crescent moon this city is named after. I want to tell him something important as I hear him slap & slap the animal, first soft like a clap during service's joy, then hard like a stomp during service's dances until a loud smack like when I've been bad.

Above me, mumbling close to my face, his voice is scratchy like when he sings to Muddy Waters & Louis. Everything looks foggy, sounds like gargling. He says Noah would never have saved a sinner like me. I should stop my crying, start swimming so the great river can see me & keep me from going under, down where our house & car are taken back by the Almighty. Then I hear a trumpet warming up. A hungry noise, a gator's open-teeth snap. I breathe & breathe & obey for the love of God, the way Isaac did with his eyes closed, without murmuring, aware of the sharp steel but not what his father hears, what his father knows, yet still willing to go through the floating door.

Response to: Step on a Crack

Every kid knew the legends, how Jimmy's mama said she slid on ice, her legs scooped skyward, defying gravity, until shriek-thud. Her bones slipped out of place, her back broken. Hard to say anything about the shiner. *Put the blame on Jimmy,* they taunted, *step on a crack, break your mama's back.* Father finger pointed to Jimmy, but clipboards kept coming, forms needed filling, boxes required checking. Father rode in a red-wailing car. The world felt surreal & nothing seemed the same. Worse, the rest of summer turned lame. Kids stopped playing on their side of the block. Grandma came over a lot more, while mama moved in her chair slow-slow, that she painted tortoise-green, moving-green, new-room green. Out in the woods, cousin Judy made him cry, claiming his Father would never come back before she twirled & sang in falsetto

Jimmy steps on a crack, breaks his mama's back.
His Daddy hit her because he's a little shitter.

This made his cheeks hot & he wanted to pop her in the mouth to shut that trap. It was Grandma who set him straight later that night after the bedtime ritual of reading. She was in the middle of a fairy tale, something about a forest & being lost. His mind drifted, waiting to ask about the earlier event. *Oh, Jimmy, those are just folks telling tales. Not long ago, we thought the number of cracks meant the number of china dishes we would break before the sun set.* He didn't really know this "superstition"; sounded like someone patching up a large hole or hemming up new pants with mama's super stitchin'. Restless, he dreamed about snow & sharp shards. At his new school, his teacher with the name that sounded close to old-bird warned if kids stepped on the cracks in the street, they would get eaten by bears waiting around corners for a small snack to walk by & the thought of Judy being devoured by these bears made him feel just right inside.

COKELORE

To prove it was true, Matt did what his scientist dad would do with a theory & pulled his loose front tooth to put it in a cup of coke, sacrificing the pillow money which would have gone toward another Star Wars comic book or for a TIE fighter, the space ship he wanted but never got for his birthday. At bedtime, he took an hour to fall asleep, knowing the tooth would dissolve, proving the babysitter wrong. He wasn't sure why it mattered that the babysitter knew he was right but the way his tummy stirred at the thought, he knew it did.

A soft bump-bump in the night woke him & he threw the covers back, flipped the nightstand light on & darted toward the kitchen to check on his experiment. The tooth was still there. He big-frowned the way kids do with their whole body but then remembered dawn was hours away. Next to his Captain America glass he bought at Burger King was a half-finished bottle of beer, which he knew not to touch, & some soda in a fancy glass. It tasted different than regular soda, sweeter like movie-theater candy & it made him feel free & bouncy, astronaut-light. He headed toward the playroom to find his light saber, suddenly ready to play & run, remembering something funny from school, snorting & laughing, lacking the urge to sleep & unaware of the darkness or the lateness of the hour.

In his playroom, the babysitter wore his dress-up lab coat & his stethoscope but nothing else. She was on all fours, looking both serious & sad, while dad seemed ready to wrestle or get angry. He didn't like seeing that face. He was about to say something but couldn't remember what he was doing when everything got quiet. Nobody moved. Nobody said anything. For the first time, his dad looked frightened & his fists shook but not in their normal Hulk way. It reminded him of the posters outside the movies that made him look away & hold his dad's hand tighter, that were rated 'R' for red,
cardinal red,
stop sign red,
blood red.

Fumes

The day mama & I leave, two
Canada geese arrive—
their long, black necks arrow
toward the pond & fold into themselves
like cocktail napkins.
I hope they'll stay there
forever. The afternoon burnishes
mama from freckle-red to bruised-peach,
a glass of brewed tea
left out & discolored.
Ladybugs cling to the apple-red
of the front door, a small
mosquito meals on my arm,
& a solitary squirrel digs for nuts.

After a day of packing, she rushes
me into the car, exhaust fumes sputter
moons. This is June:
dust blots the glass,
love bugs & moths
smear the customized grill.
The car trembles with purpose.
In the back seat, I
wait. A pale blue plush
pillows my bruised head.
On the busted porch,
father crushes cans, smokes
Strikes. Mama peals away—
runs over the white mailbox.

Response to: Don't Swallow your Gum or It will Grow into a Tree

For once, mama was right & the tummy tree took root, running through my sister's body, a nightmarish version of Tai Chi as her internal energy developed during *Zhan Zhuang* into bark & trunk, twisting knots & squishing through softness, a slow, strangling snake ready to swallow the waste she'd become, twigs sprout from knuckles & break through her jail-ribs but ignore the leaking heart-sack as branches fatten & stretch skyward while leaves unfurl cocoons of foil-wrapped candy bars ready for the entire neighborhood's savage consumption until they each bloom gum ball bone & dangle cotton-candy moss forever surrounding her chewed-up altar.

Response to: Chocolate Causes Massive Acne

At first, the preteens refused to believe, but then the red bubbles spotted his face & neck, trailed down his chest snake-like & coated his body, swelling to candy shell size then puffy thin-mint circles that oozed thick white, which, of course, caused cries of surprise from his family & by the time the doctors admitted him, the acne ballooned to gumdrop size, showing no sign of stopping, & word spread until the children in town heard it from the grocer & the coffee shop lady & even the shoe store guy in the church choir. What could they do in the face of it all? After the cruel truth was known, the kids dug through their drawers & under their bed, all the nooks where they kept their secret-secrets, removing their stash of sweet treats, those half-eaten bars & the brown bags stuffed with odd bits & chunks, every piece plunked into the trash bins before they could suffer the same, have their own teen troubles begin.

Mud Man

"Speak to the earth, and it shall teach you."
—Job 12: 7-8

Needing a father, I create a *dybbuk*
of mire & soil & clay,
layered with discarded leaves
from a maple or live oak
with leaves green on one side,
packed from the seasoned bones
of extinct animals
and the rocks my daughter collects.

Together we chant our silly song:
Mud, mud, glorious mud
Nothing quite like it for cooling the blood
So follow me follow, down to the hollow
& there let me wallow in glorious mud.

When I call his name,
he bubbles to the top
like chemicals in a beaker.
When he sees me
with my daughter,
he scoops her onto shoulders
cloudy as smoke-oil,
takes us to Italian fields
filled with lavender & sunflower.

My mud man gives her all
the secrets the earth bares.
He responds to her sounds,
speaks about puddles,
how to walk without breaking twigs,
shaping dolls from reeds.
He nods with assiduous attention,
shows her where earthworms
are born, how termites travel
for food, the aureate gifts of the sun,
the wonder at a pond's bottom,
the fathomable kingdom of frogs.

Miracle

When the magic menorah first spoke, we had not even finished the blessing. Startled, mama screamed & I stared at opening & closing lips, golden, like little *latkes*. No eyes, no nose, nothing but a small mouth centered on the candelabra's throat, the *Shamash* that stands above the rest. The two blue candles burned their swift dance. The dining room clock chimed the hour. No one ran or called the cops; this was not some B movie. We sat & listened. It spoke Hebrew we only half understood like a Friday night service but with an old European accent. When it smoked out & the oozed wax had pooled & froze at the base's bottom, we faced each other with a renewed sense of life's little wonders, having heard a Godly wisdom. We stayed up late, too excited to sleep. Mama made a pot of decaf with the French press & we played family games, laughing & smiling, high on our own love. We went to bed without opening any presents. In the morning, when we retold what happened to our neighbor, Mr. Levine, to the Rabbi, to the visiting cantor, to the men's club, to the local paper, to a pair of radio DJs & to anyone we met throughout the day, no one ever asked us what the menorah meant, what the menorah said.

Miracle Shoes
—United States Holocaust Memorial Museum

One day, the stacked shoes begin to rise
  leisurely, puppets on strings.
At first people pour into the museum
  to view the shoes floating about.
A curtain drawn back,
  a chamber unlocked,
  the shoes silently sweep through the air
  like Astaire & Rogers.
The watchers whisper & point, gasp
  & stare. The murmurs ache
  with melody, violins in a symphony.
A girl in a green dress
  thinks the shoes are waltzing
  & the newspapers take to it,
  begin referring to them
  as Little Dancers—
laces like wired shadows.

Soon the other exhibits go unnoticed.
A few people gather outside
  with candles & army-surplus blankets,
  singing songs about being saved
  & chanting prayers in unison.
This goes on for many nights
  & everyone who hears them
  is filled with a solemn beauty.
Some weep & others make silent vows.

Early on a Saturday in September,
  an old security guard, coffee cup in hand
  & *The Post* tucked under his arm,
  holds the heavy doors open
  a little too long,
  & the shoes start to slip through,
a ballet of swirling, hovering couples.
Later, he will be quoted
  as saying he never did spill
  a damn drop of coffee
  or ruin his paper.
Never did he think
  about closing that door.

Sitting in a Simulated Space at the Atlantic Station IKEA in Atlanta, Georgia
for James Wright

Overhead dangles a spinning butterfly, glittering blue on a plastic trunk. I sit comfortably on a cushioned chair tucked into a specially designed desk that unfolds like wooden origami. I'm reading poems by an author I don't know off a shelf with a name I can't pronounce. I find myself ripping out two pages, stifling the urge to plagiarize a line about the moon & how the slender echo of light we see is not real but still true, true in the sense anything can be, until I see a little girl wearing a worn skirt spotted with cows & bells, a girl who looks nothing like my own, that is to say everything like my daughter, who stares at my crime the way kids stare at difference, while she tugs & tugs at her father's shirt cuff.

***

This could be my own house & my own room with my easy-to-assemble furniture & carefully arranged knickknacks of Eiffel Towers & replica planes, surrounded by piles of books in carefully-planned staircase stacks about Swedish sunsets, Swedish architecture & a Swedish poet or two, books that are no different than my own coffee table books I've never read, that is to say nothing like my own books, for this is the better, brighter version of me where everything is new & clean.

***

Between all this paper & plastic & rows of replication I think about life, that is to say shopping, how it is simply getting into a big box store, meandering to the middle the way one might row to the center of a lake or pond, some body of dark water only to start sinking while only half-way out.

I decide it's time to move on & stroll to the next room. I spot another compact desk beneath a small shelf with wicker baskets great for any space, perfect for a condo I don't own & an over-sized chair on wheels, which I want to own the way I would like to have it all somehow fit into my cul-de-sac house, a place that has never been this inviting, this perfect.

***

To my right, a picture of lavender fields stretching for sunlight between two dirt roads to remind us that this room is exotic, romantic even, & all we have to do to achieve this sense of times past, this feeling of wonderment one can only find in yesterday's gone or in rural lands, lands where horses still clump along, is to tell ourselves, it can all be had, it can all be yours, & like a daily mantra we repeat before our morning coffee & cream-filled donuts, we tell ourselves to stop wasting these moments, this opportunity already at a deep discount, to do the right thing & just charge it. I pull out my worn wallet & head for the exit to my right in *a field of sunlight between two pines.*

Response to: You're Going to Dig a Hole to China

If you're reading this, you know the whole incident is classified, can't talk about it. Sealed lips, signed forms. The works. In fact, this is "fiction". For the dog & my kid, well, let's just say it's a dream, the ones where you know you're in a dream but you go with it anyway because waking up is more trouble & really you're still tired. I should mention, sometimes the neighbors came over on Sunday afternoon when it was our day to fire up the BBQ, bring out the dogs & turn small-talk into art. The kids would all scramble about, an organized fire crew sliding up & down the embankment, enjoying the moment, making mountains out of molehills, literally. Listen, I know the newspapers need their stories, had their fun at our expense, but honestly there was nothing better than standing on flagstone, flipping burgers, breaking out a twelve pack, & watching all the kids & a few fathers scurry meerkat-like, filled with determination & joy for the moment. Make no mistake, "nothing" happened. How did it end up, you ask? The way all memories do, muddled with those little pleasurable points in time, the ones where we remember reaching over to our significant other, one hand on a shoulder or caressing hair, faces full of smiles for our life together, when sex meant sharing not warfare, before the lawyers & their blue pens, before weekend events became caught in the shadows of work-long weekdays, before we dug ourselves out of that muddy cul-de-sac hole.

"I Don't Believe," She Said, "In You."

With two words, it happened jackrabbit fast, an idea darting under the shrub & away from the speeding light, swirling into the heavy distance, a spell cast, a cause deserted. *I don't believe you. I don't believe you.* She stared incredulous, wide-eyed, with one hand on her hip & her left hand opened, ready to stop something larger than this moment, the heart's barrier, a dream catcher of flesh & bone & nail. *I. Don't. Believe. You.* He listened the way a child presses an ear to a keyhole, carrying a sense of magic & the impossible into a room caught in darkness where some sound could mean mermaid, could mean dragon. He heard her. He heard the loose strand of hem, the eye lid's extra blink, the let loose arrow a mile away. He heard in you. *In you.*

Response to: It's Getting Harder & Harder to Leave the House

Yes, but think how difficult it is for the house, always missing you, always waiting, thankless, unnoticed, untouched, under-appreciated, so sometimes, yeah, the house wishes it could leave, just for a day mind you, growing brick boat shoes or nimble wooden limbs, anything to ease into a journey of adventure away from rodents, peeing pets, & other pests living off its flaking skin—oh, let's not forget the humans who sponge away its soul, spending time slipping away to other houses & dreaming of faraway homes, homes that float at the edge of exotic wonderlands more hut than safe enclosure, homes no one abandons or forecloses, homes full of bowl-candy love everyone finds too-damn-happy to forget much less leave.

Bait & Trap

From my fingers,
I peel the frayed fabric
of my skin.
I can't resist tugging
at the seam,
the hound dog pointer
sniffs our flakes
& loose strands.
The pain of the long strip
baits me every time
& I imagine myself a mummy,
discovering myself—

but I like to feel the ache,
watch the shine swell up,
bull's-eye red.
I am a zombie to my urges.
But this is a bear trap,
where I pick-ax tap
gnaw & claw, attempting
to mine down
to the heart of the problem,
searching for some treasure
I never see.
I won't stop
until I find the blue river
peaking from the ice.
I never make it.
The pain always becomes
too much & I stop.

But I don't want to stop.
I want to eat away
this paper-mâché wrap
& unmask the perfect body beneath.

Response to: Why Don't You Just Get Outta Here

Sometimes an idea begins with a simple question, a wave of a hand, dismissing you like the half-hearted swipe of a nearby fly. But this time the idea makes sense the way we believe invisibility is a power we want to have. Look there is a pool—jump in, sink down, look around. You are just organs & sacs of fat, spaces that sway like the sea. Don't they see? You are tired of being seen by their dissecting eyes, sharp & bold. Water lets you forget everything dry & everything that can touch—except above you, a small assembly line of folks are pointing down, flailing their hands at your defiant act. It always begins with pointing. They are pointing the way he points. It is different but it is the same. They blame you because he smiles & you do not. Today, they are distorted fish & you are cocooned in a drowning dream. That was a lie. The fish are sharks & everyone is hungry. Too late: you have already been a take-out meal. *Give me a break* they say, *stop lying. Stop being a child.* It doesn't matter that you have crooked teeth or dull eyes more blue than this pool, that your body is shaped by appetite & by magazines that teach you what to love & how. You don't have to read them anymore. How many minutes do you have left? You want the metallic taste. You thirst for it in a way they don't see. Take a minute to contemplate the thin slice of absence, the meaning of sinking & draining, how confusing a smile is, & how it only takes a few seconds for us to easily mix up cold for warm, yes for no, or a piece of hello for a peaceful goodbye.

Response to: I Can't Get Off the Couch

Face it, the couch can't get away from you, no matter how hard it tries to be a wallflower, to simply enjoy the space & its place in the room rather than worry about stubs for legs & unmoving arms, the shadows that cobweb corners, the hours spent lost in darkness, dreaming *feng shui,* but waking with a load of water, those sacks stuck in their flaky skin who are busy staring at bright boxes full of unimaginable action & aching hearts. Look, the couch would love nothing more than to waste the day caped with a shawl, laying burdened on someone's back like Atlas, but honestly the couch is waiting for the right cover to turn it almost youthful & beautiful, waiting for the vibrating wonder of the vacuum so it can come clean, eyeing the shapely Victorian curves of the love-seat, waiting & waiting for it to make the first move.

Returning to the Abortion Clinic
Houston, TX 1998

In a place built for waiting women,
we watch two men carry away
the ceiling-high fountain,
leaving a vast space
where that trickling once existed
in the center of the room,
full of those eager for news,
good or bad,
where flipping pages
& the click-click of knitting needles
is now a perpetual tuning
for an absent symphony.

Silence would be better.

Sitting near the exit,
a girl whose name I forget
with bird eyes & wish bone legs
readies herself to leave.
She's afraid to take off her coat
& expose her belly's burden
but suffering from warmth.

To avoid agonizing
about the paper dress
& everything that goes with it,
I chatter about the weather, our finals
& the two it took
to take the spitting angel
away, whether they knew
what the constant, giddy-like burbling
meant to us in a room so cramped,
so carelessly created for waiting.

Menorah-Mama at Mt. Sinai

Metal arms, octopus-long,
        suck & hiss,
move machine-heavy
in a room built for snoring.

        Nothing makes sense.
Mama has become a *menorah*.
Her body tries to make
              its own miracle.

        Matching our tired eyes,
she flickers with fear.
        I want to lick the oil
from her thin, black hair.

Torn by tradition
        & her present condition, we stand
unprepared for the confusion.
We wait with the whole family

        for comfort. They give her
a place in the corner
where walls glow white,
              a desert sun, a beacon of false hope.

        Someone in charge speaks
well rehearsed Latin. Mumbo gumbo.
        We don't know what to feel,
filling the space with stories

about the night of the wobbly mantle
        & the bug-bitten Sabbath,
or the evening we used our gas stove
on the candles when we lost

   the lighter box. We move through
the holiday routine
& mention our best menorah memories
   as we praise her,

   shine her up,
a top-shelf trophy.
   No one says fever
or lesions.

Step-Dad sits with us
   on the other bed.
We play a few games.
We sing some songs, stopping

   to eat chocolate *gelt*
until my sister asks for *latkes*,
which makes mama cry.
   From her nose, snot drips

   like melting wax.
We forget to say the Hebrew.
   We forget to open our gifts.
At dawn,

before we have to go,
   before we know what to do,
we linger long enough
to watch her burn & puff out.

Dear Sister Dreydel,

Tell me how this happened, what went wrong?
Before we knew the signs, to be on watch,
you swallowed a Dreydel, a wooden one,
the size of a radish. This ancient tool for learning,
now a holiday toy, became your nickname.
The babysitter often stared at corners,
worrying about where the toy went
& worse, how it got out.
Yes, some mysteries are
better left alone.
Once you ate a cactus, soil & all.
By age three, your tongue turned blue
for ten days before the berry-pit red
returned. Mother found the remains
of an ink pad in her art drawer.
They began to suspect you hungered
for color when the following summer
you beheaded the doctor's prized Mammoth Sunflowers.
In third grade, your teacher noticed missing bonsai buds.
We began to laugh less & wonder more.

You withdrew from playtime, shrank
from anything gentle. How did your need
for understanding in a world hardly
black-&-white become violent?
By fourteen, you broke into houses
to cut cords from neighbor's phones.
You punched stacked melons in the neighborhood grocer,
cursed nuns at the local kitchen,
even pushed one down a flight of stairs.
That summer, you failed
several attempts to out siren a cop car.
Drugs & shrinks were useless.
Therapy tore you down—
didn't keep you too submerged

from trouble. By high school,
you immersed yourself
in street shadows, spinning more & more
out of control, giving money
to anyone who asked
but looked for shortcuts to get more.

    ***

Many mornings you search for a way
to measure emotions, to explore meaning
behind simple smiles, to decode the language
of shrugs & gestures. You can't
read eyes or understand faces.
You never see light's pulse in hair, never
the stars in eyes or when they change
from skyglow to gun-dark.

    ***

You still collect museums of marbles
in mason jars & a universe of new pennies
in another you call starshine.
You steal strings of gold
from neighbors, try to swallow
a few to feel the shimmer.
You gulp our cousin's goldfish
into your mouth but reject any pills
that could help. After a few years, doctors
stop making marks in files
& nurses note more gauze,
more places to patch.
After two decades, we agree
without saying so
to give up, giving in to a system
of tough-love shelters
drowning in grave-gray.

How to explain your disorder
to your left behind baby?
Our shrink said you're a deep sea diver
always in darkness, & your mind:
a sunken ship.
Do you see how this happened?
What went wrong?
Tell me. I'm ready to listen.
Tell me. Where do you sleep,
why do you refuse
aid? Tell me
what you crave.

Final Exam

"Feet, why do I need you when I have wings to fly?"
—Frida Kahlo

Late afternoon, too late for a full walk around the man-made lake, too hot for a real run, I pause where birds busy being birds & light. I feel large, a survivor with Resheph's arrow a shallow nick in my thyroid, still aglow with radiation & the doctor's news. After having walked on fire, fought a microscopic menace, I see pulses, feel a part of the whole, a surge of energy that charges life—except off the path, a bird, black with sun's shimmer-streaks & two feet, oddly bent, trying to take flight, twitching its head side to side, unable to break gravity's barrier, blinking, blinking at me as it persists, tries to flap, awaiting the magic, the grace once granted. Now nothing.

I watch the struggle, caught by the helpless horror, the poor bird's keen mewl as it falls back onto useless feet, urgent to take to the spaces above. For some reason, I poke it with the tip of my shoe to see what it would do, but it does not peck or cry out, so I try to force flight by scooping the bird, a living soccer ball, that lands on a patch of brown grass. Our eyes both show fear for what must come next, for the choice I cannot yet make, to kill or not to kill, to save & doctor, cost aside, or let death run its course?

Endings
after A.M.

What do I know of endings when in winter
I'm not alone? Sometimes I forget this togetherness
in all this rural silence, ignore the language
of dogwood & bare oak,
their leaves glazed on my lot, sprinkled
with the neighbor's acorn crunch.
Frost's foil wraps on the bones
of house & yard alike. We live so fast
we let slip this topography
we share, the small tracks of birds
passing through on their way
to paradise where skies whistle
or hum. But when no cars
or people pass by, it's easy
to think this place is the land
of ghosts & savage smoke,
where each step crinkle-cracks
as feet push down & the snow
gives way. But we are not
abandoned by shine & shimmer,
stuck between shades of mountain,
condemned to a barren stretch
of quiet plains. A harsh breeze,
if you look long enough,
is choreography, & a skein of geese
can be the exposition, not the final act.
Those barred stars above
are not more gray; clouds break
apart & push along. We can be open arms,
our own light, a threshold to beauty.
The distant bright is a gate,
& if you see it, you know we choose
our locks; we create our paths.

Meditation before Falling Asleep

Sometimes I lay back in a light jacket, black
with the hood pulled down
over temple, brow & my eyes.

I wait for the moments before sleep,
for the dark blur
of quiet.

Like a vampire, I cross
my arms,
afraid of light.

I drain the day away
until empty, empty as the space
behind an ambulance.

Finding my Father's Kinnor

When they break open my father's lungs like a pistachio,
they find his kinnor still strung.

The soundboard has grown into bone,
five times the size it used to be.

The two arms that extend
parallel to the instruments body

are now his arms,
not the mangled ones

crushed by that sleeping man
in a red-light running truck.

I was not there.
I was late.

I sneak into his autopsy,
a mask over my face

like the one I always wear,
& when the ten strings once made from sheep's small intestine

start to sing,
we become haunted

by this absence of hollow,
by this inner beauty.

So they stand, knife in hand,
happily amazed,

while I admire his arms
that look thick & strong,

like stone, heavy enough
to lift me back into his song.

Finding the Perfect Tune for the Last

i.
With earphones on, you scan for the perfect song,
a song that says this is who I want to be,
but no note is perfect, no song can know
the wings caught in your ribs,
the fluttering prayer in your chest,
how sometimes, sky can break bones
& wind can eat light,
absorbed like an unborn twin.
This might be your last.
Why not? Everyone gets one
instrument of their choosing,
one note that says it all,
trying to echo
the moon's mezzo-forte,
but settling
for the pianissimo of sand.

ii.
Within the birdcage of your ribs,
kicks & flaps a White-lined Sphinx Moth
made from your cosmic cell.
You tell me you don't believe
in this poetic nonsense,
that a body is a body
& a star is far away
in cloud-locked skies.

I want to free this *hummingbird moth*,
majestic & large,
an American giant.

I want to be born
with birdsongs bubbling in my chest,
chosen & hungry for what this land has to offer,

to let them loose,
like crayons & cookies,
to hear their song,
songs made for the living,
songs made for trees & silver dew.

iii
I want to die away
from schools stained with these little lasts,
where hearing just one child cry
can be wordless joy,
& yes, it is cliché & broken,
a mixed up tune
that's sadness & relief—
a little girl, your boy—

                        this diminishes us.
It's too much to speak plain.
It's just too much.
Your child is dead, mine
is alive,
so beautifully alive,
the way a dry fountain
can still hold coins,
while sharp-eyed birds are browsing by,
flying the way birds can,
looking to take the shine away.

You can't hear this last
in front of a screen, playing your game,
playing your songs that make it easy
to forget these little blips, these birds of light,
but trust me when I say you who congregate here
between these lines, these cocooned rows,
that there is so much buried light—
there really is—but you
don't know how to make it fire.

Friday at Publix in Atlanta

At checkout, a tall man in an overcoat
stands with two kids,
one in each tight hand.
The store is crowded.
Everyone has dinner to make,
company to keep.
My cart looks deep
and hollow, one frozen meal,
a bottle of soda, and a bar
of chocolate. The woman,
getting checked out by an old grocer,
is half my age, buttoned
in a yellow parka
like a ripe banana.

I almost laugh—
except her cart is flowing
with cans and meals and sweets.
She must have a lover
and two or three kids,
a mini van, washed and bright
as stars. She sings showtunes
on the way to her two story home,
hopes she has time for her yoga class,
hopes all is safe and right.

Out of the corner of my eye,
I see a kid wiggle free
to touch an impulse item
while the Dad seizes the moment
to check stocks or sports
on his new phone.
I pretend not to hear
when the grocer pauses
to let me know the self-checkout

is free. I think *no rush*.
She points a puffy finger
my way. I avoid eye contact
until she resumes
the blips and beeps,
a steady sound
of something achieved.

II

"Men love a prop so well, that they will lean on a pointed poisoned spear."

—Mary Shelley, *The Last Man*

Love Poem for Wings

At first, they felt heavy & sore
like new boots but with a constant itch.
Feathers, silky but stiff,
left mica dust flecks.
Almost sweaty & dizzy,
I almost crumpled under their weight.
When they brushed my cheek,
it tickled & sometimes
gave a static shock.

My first love saw their steady flutter
& blushed with bedroom thoughts.
After we explored each other's bodies,
she said they shimmered brighter than an oyster's nacre
with a hint of orchids & spring rain.
At night when the moon was mine
& the hungry wind held me high,
I knew I could never
be grounded again.

Mud Angel

Earth. Nothing more. / Earth. Nothing less. / And let that be enough for you.
—Pedro Salinas

In the barn, he removes
& folds his clipped wings,

a blue-gray, not from dye
but from age, grime, storage.

Gently, the bruised feathers
brush the scar on his left cheek.

At night, in flight,
it itches more

like a healing wound
open to air. Every morning,

every morning he looks down
from the loft, rests

a hand on a bale of hay,
thinks about chores

& closes the trunk, thick
with dust & dirt,

then turns, his back bare
with phantom limbs.

Undone

While walking & talking about dinosaurs,
who wonders about absence,
whether their death
will be handfuls,
big scoops of grief?

You have to know how extinction feels—now.
I stand on a hill of daffodils
looking down at the swaying yellow bells
that touch you

& it makes my eyes tear:
on your back, arms folded,
stiff, seeing how far the earth

will take you—even now,
as darkness reaches down

to meet you, my child,

    I watch you play dead,

    holding your beautiful breath

    until a puff bursts free.

The Mermaid Meets Mud Angel

"Wheat fields up as far as the hills, boundless as the ocean, delicate yellow, delicate soft green, the delicate purple of a tilled and weeded piece of ground, with the regular speckle of the green of flowering potato plants, everything under a sky..."

—Van Gogh in his last letter to his Mother, painting: <u>Wheat Field under Clouded Skies, 1890</u>

1. Lure

In wheat fields up as far as the hills,
she follows a newly made path
with streaks of dried mud,
broken twigs & bits of fluff,
white as hope.

She steps around torn petals
from flowers, *delicate yellow,*
delicate soft green,
makes her way
toward a wheat field,
swaying in Spring,

boundless as the ocean. A blue
button-eye scarecrow points to an altar
made of pink coral, seashells
of all sizes & driftwood,
carved with small flying fish.

How many months
to drag the wood here, to build this
lure? Surely, no man *tilled & weeded,*
planned it with so much patience,
with so much grace?

2. Leaves & Roots

She longs for the cocoon of constant sea—even while walking in pastures flamed with tulips, daffodils & red-leafed shrubs. She dreams of kelp kissing her hair as she swirls with the seals, where little fish clean & massage & salt swoons through her. Yet she left these wonders for this sun-worn land, packed tight with skyscrapers that make her head spin. Worse, spaces are the spaces swarming with leaves & roots.

3. Ripples

She never intended to stay,
to lay with a man more majestic
than whale songs,
more restless than sharks.
But his pale eyes
sparkled like scales,
his touch rippled,
& his breath in her ear
was a riptide.

"For you", he says,
"everything under a sky."

4. Snake Wind

On a black sand beach, he vows to find fields to harvest, builds a farmhouse to confine the way his father showed him. The first time he leaves
for "much needed supplies", she soaks in shade, stretches her arms out in the tickle of tall grass, listens to the wind's hiss & thinks she does not want the secrets of the ocean floor.

Song birds & crows land near, eyeing bugs—she dreams crowds of corn, beans & golden grains, stalks standing together like a regiment waiting for defeat. Rolling onto her side, she grabs a red rock from the ground: a fat-tailed flatness, burnt brown spots. She thinks about how it sits, light touching its back, shrinking to sand specks, noting nothing. Above her: mindless moss, a bland tree. Beneath her: pulsing yard. Among the flowering potato plants, gnats descend toward her spot. Before long, the day slips away like shed skin.

5. The Fishermen Mystic with the Old White Robe

For answers to this longing,
she drives to the harbor,
finds a fisherman with a face
like nori. He offers her fugu,
half-smiles when spoken to,
pretends he does not know
her questions, her metaphors,
her frustration.

His arms are taut,
bites & bumps riddle his legs.
She learns the benefits of baiting,
how to strive for a good catch,
& uses for the whole.

Sometimes he wears an old robe,
recites recipes, laughs like a dolphin,
reads Neruda, Lo & Bashō
in languages she does not know.

One day, he ceases mid-
sentence. Hungry

for apples & honey in curry rice,
a side of *rakkyo* pickles,
for paths up a winding, solitary trail.
perplexed, she follows a few feet behind.
The morning sun blinds,
but she follows.

When they reach a creek
full of women washing clothes & men
casting hand-made rods,
she is too far behind.
He disappears
into a stream of natives,
where the water around his feet
has been moving for centuries.

6. Ending on a Line from Rilke

Creating wreaths from quills, vines & lavender, she decorates the
windows, waits for his return. No one believes her. Chickens freely
wander through the house. Overgrown with waist-high weeds, the coop
has lost heat. She talks to herself about a flying man
who took her high in the sky & left her with child. She picks needle-like
herbs, braids sage with rosemary: cooks some & with the rest, creates
figurines of angels, makes paint out of berries & yucca plants. Some
days to repay favors, she builds rustic bird cages with wood piled for
the barn. She hears the surf break in her cupboard, & in her hearth,
sirens. Sometimes she scoops mouthfuls of dirt to remember his scent;
sometimes she forgets the day, loses her way in her own house.

7. Winter Morning

A bungalow bedroom window ricochets
the dawn with dim light. A woman moves about,
mumbles about her sea-faring days. The blue flame sighs.
The red kettle sits, waits for the right moment—slowly
speaks back. Even the kettle knows
sorrow's sound.

8. Epilogue

After weeks, the town no longer laughs when she stops bathing or squawks at birds & dances at the county fair with no pants. They begin to wonder if something inside her bones has failed, that there must be "a leak in the thatch of her head" when she says his eyes glow like viperfish at night during flight. The church no longer leaves small baskets of food & supplies. The ladies' club drives on by. Friends refuse to call, to lend their hands, to continue to care for someone who waits for the impossible, when the field rots, when roots remain famished & birds soar past to where other combines grind, where irrigation keeps the earth filled with worms & abundance.

They tire from hearing her rants about the sea, the tale about his honeyed hair & flies higher than hawks. On most mornings, when the night vanishes into her eyes, she looks to the horizon, hums fragments of songs in a language long dead, then checks her trap: the hole, the net, the rope threaded with gold. She listens to the lull of the creek, counts the constellations in the sky's dim pit.

Sea Watching

On a turtle beach
crunching with shells,

> water drifts slowly
> past a ribbon of shore.

Gawkers go to help
hatchlings. A dead man's wife

> walks in his favorite flip-flops,
> two sizes too big.

She uses driftwood for a crutch,
not quite lost,

> pausing by the rock wall,
> where children climb & play,

where sand dollars stay hidden
& where crabs scurry about

> filling themselves
> with algae & death.

Under a full moon, she takes her time
meandering, unraveled

> by loss's loose strands.
> She waits nine months for the sea

to bring back
something green.

Secret Wings

i

No longer floating,
his wings covered
with salt,
Papa moves
as a shade.
He hums fragments
of forgotten songs,
remembers nothing
of being beneath the heavens,
having settled
for fertile ground & hot meals.

Now he knows what his family knows:
the dirt, the plow, the same field
as his father's. He dreams crowds
of corn, beans, grains, stalks
standing together like a regiment.

He envies the new moon,
how nothing moves
slower than change,
& he scratches the dust
from his face, presses
his back to the barn
like a black bear
who shakes for an itch.

Under his chipped & chewed
fingernails, he toils tomorrow
with soil & grease & worry,
never raising his beaten fists
to punch the sky.

    Let him eat mud if he must,
    let him put his mouth to it,
    hands in puddles, head bent,
    so there may be harvest.

ii

Born in a field of soft dirt,
I learn not to want aloud, not here
in the garden I sow, not here

where this dust-caked child
can't ask a thing:
    why Papa bites his nails,
    where Papa hid his wings.

The Patience Stone at the Mobile Mini Children's Circus in Kabul

Come closer. Tell me why you do what you do. I'm all ears & if I had a mouth, who would I tell? I hear stories, know sorrows. Of course, I keep them safe. Here at the Children's Circus, I listen to complaints, worries, dreams unfulfilled. But then you two arrive, daughter thrilled by the exhibits, amazed by the sad cages that tame anything wild, the wonders they could've been. You both pick me, the tallest pillar painted blue; *sea-blue,* she says, letting go of your hand to whisper kid concerns. *Secret-blue,* you think. A lone bird passes over head. The heat makes you thirsty. She leans in & masks her mouth, two-handed. You cannot hear her. You have spent all day trying to explain you won't move with her to Israel & abandon the dusty backstreets, the thin Poplar trees, the cold sweetness of *falooda* you buy at the corner market, the bakery that sold *Afghan Bread* to your father & your father's father. It's your turn. I am ready. Your back faces your child; your eyes barely see me. You don't lean toward me or cup your hands. You say what you came to say, loud & afraid. I can't help but wonder if this will be the last one, the one that will finally cause me to crack & crumble, allow these secrets to swirl upward, whirling in the wind, rising past the blue until it seals a shooting star's fissure.

Spaces

      A father stands at the train station
& sees the spaces   further down the tracks,

         stares at everything moving away,
reminds him of the Ferris wheel

    near the circus,
the one that   starts slowly

        but seems to speed up
& rock near the top.

     He imagines the spokes flying by
until they waver   & bend light,

        catching time,
one container stuck at the second highest point,

    boxed within
two passengers: a mother & daughter.

       They push their arms upward,
laughing loudly, eating air,

     making the gondola sway even more,
a moment   they do not want to end.

       He signals farewell to this train
that carries those he loves,

    almost as much as his cause,
almost   as much as staying,

     & while his wife will not wave,
eyes full of lost futures,

          his daughter does, believing
in something that   will not happen,

                all grins
& wind-loose hair,

           believing this train
is   a ride

                that will return them
to where they began.

Imaginary Prop List for an Abandoned Temple

Bucket for debris,
    broom & new paint,
                bits & chips
            of imported stained glass,
        a miracle that puzzles it whole,
a scene from Moses, Noah,
    the favorites, five books
                wrapped with care, lavish,
        near a small container of oil,
        always full, always lit, always constant,
call it eternal, the beginnings of a prayer,
    where the rabbi imagines
                people, people sitting in seats,
        people rising,
        rising to fill this hungry house.

On the Sixth Day

Under a new roof in a new land, his wife & daughter kiss the *mezuzah*, stand on a doormat bright with leaves, a fearful joy in their eyes, breaths full of morning tea, cheese, bread & olive. A screen door bangs its wooden drum.

He refuses to feel this sand & salt air, how autumn grabs their hair in play. His family watches wind snag the Almond tree, the falling shells knock on stubborn earth, ready for the new next, the bloom & buzz that will rise & follow frost.

The Last Jew

Zablon Simintov, the last Jew in Afghanistan since 2005

i.

Sometimes we all feel like you,
>a single stick in a rushing river.
>Honestly, who has not felt
>hairs rise on the base of our neck
>when hands cup to other ears
>full of distressing whispers?

You could be in Calcutta or Krakow,
>any place given to time
>for those *olim* who made *aliyah*.
>"Next year in Jerusalem"
>they said dutifully
>until they did.

Today you are the Last
>Jew, the chosen carpet dealer
>in the heart of Kabul
>where Hebrew letters breathe
>into morning birds,
>where echoes sink in
>surrounding streets,
>unswept rooms & broken glass,
>an eerie emptiness,
>a staleness under cracked fans
>& dusty cupboards, empty
>of books, hundreds
>of years old, where God

grumbles to you & you alone.

Every Friday night,
>the missing make a slight noise,
>the shuffling hush of leaves,
>the slow slipping drip of sand,
>the first open beat of wing,
>all fluttering echoes of sky.

ii.

Do you hoist the Torah
        above your shoulders, bear it
        around the sanctuary for ghosts
        to touch it with their *tallises*?
        On the Sabbath, do you kiss
        the book? Recite the prayers?

Whom do you preach to? Who in your synagogue is teaching?

I don't know why I'm still living here.
        To anyone who cares,
        you say the reason you stay, avoid
        seeing your wife
        for over a decade
        is "God's will," but when

Moses confronted the pharaoh
        or when Abraham left his home in Ur,
        God never instructed them to become
        locust living off what the land offers,
        to abandon their family.
        While you wonder, you watch, you wait. Today

you are the Last Jew.

Love Poem for Land Lines

Do you remember the sound
of old phones.
The real bell ring
down those long,
Twinkie-yellow hallways
to grab the last reverberation
by the bedside
that snake of cord
connecting rooms
with the dangle
of live wire hiss,
the overlap shade chatter,
that static comfort
that felt familiar,
full of potential.

So much potential.
Solid & reassuring,
it shakes with joy,
shifting from that high-pitch sound,
excited even with a wrong number
or the glowing hum of dead air,
the call that means nevermind
but still promising.

Isn't it better
than the modern echo seeping
from a digital shell,
a tone we forget
with our own
hollow hello?

The Last Jew's Wife

The day he wished her gone he saw the table where they sat, empty, near the two water marks & the huge blot, the burnt circle in the middle made by her first stew, stained black with splotches of rust-like brown from first anniversary, when a good meal meant music & laughter & sex, but now the middle is worn by weight, by years of plates & fat pots, by heat & blemishes from meat & pasta & god-knows-what, the endless scraping, the scratches, the splinters, corners chipped & rubbed soft, the time spent polishing with turpentine mixed with two ounces of beeswax to bring the luster back, the history of a family, forgotten moments gone like the woman who wished to be as centered as this table.

The Last Days of the Balkh Bastan (2013)

He pockets his *kippah* before
entering his café,
where metal chairs no longer
fill with foreigners & soldiers.

Descending the stained stairs,
he unlocks the storage room,
flicks on the fan, warms
one of the five stoves.

A radio perched on a shelf,
left on too low to distinguish song
from static, begins to babble news
in a country where every street has something to report.

The green walls creak
with time. He wipes the skewers
& readies the space
for the Muslim cooks.

The kebab café will soon shut down.
The city's hotels are hollow.
The catering has declined. Everyone is scared
to leave his home.

He stays in his homeland,
reads from the country's last Torah
stored in a brown box
under his bed.

He prays, eats, lives
alone. Zablon Simintov
will never leave
the last *shul* in Kabul,

where he displays dog-eared
posters, dust-coated books,
& an unused *shofar*
on one of the few places

not covered with black grime.
Tomorrow, on Flower Street,
he'll wipe the fluted-iron door
laden with *Magen Davids*—

under a depilated dome,
where he hopes
the valley will once again
bloom suns.

Yellow

after Robert Dana

Today I feel like the last Jew
There is no one left

No one to say *Shalom*
Always the same

Streets with cracks
Cautions as long as legs

As legs, gardens on fire
Escapes   a newsstand, a tobacco shop

A liquor store, the blinking

Caution light that casts sounds
From inside oyster shell walls

Where cops cruise through
Faster than ambulances

More red than blue
A row of boarded buildings

Petite holes like deaf ears
This lemon-squeeze flat

Fourth floor walk-up
Drawers full of culinary dreams

A kitchen of fruit flies
Rice-puff ceilings the color of squash

Dark droppings & you
Pearl-blue phone calling for a moonlit taxi.

Imaginary Stage for an Abandoned Temple

For the final act,
the stage requires few props:
> a metal barrier around the *bima*,
> gold-colored carpet, torn chunks
> scattered around an empty ark,
> missing five scrolls
> stolen by the Taliban,
> a ram's horn,
> unused, shelved below
> an outdated calendar,
> dust & dirt & debris,
> one man, memories
> of a wife, their daughter,
> a group gathered together,

singing the same song,
singing to voices
too far to hear.

The Last Synagogue

The house of God
Inhales sand, breathing,

Breathing
Still, a low snore,

A soft rumble,
Surprising the neighbors.

While vendors & traffic
In the setting sun's empty hour

Zoom by, angry bees
Drone by, haunted

By duty
& tradition,

Where one rabbi remains,
Sermon ready.

Like keys in a pocket
Rattling & ready to go,

The house shifts
Sluggish,

Exhales amber light, lush
As New Year honey.

The Last Jew Celebrates the New Year with his Dead Friend, Ishaq Levin

After seven years,
he digs him up
for the High Holy Holidays,
brings him home
to the space they once shared,
slaps him down
in a borrowed rocker
in the empty café.

Levin, quite dead,
sways under the fan,
notices the emptiness,
says little.

Zablon, the last Jew,
thinks it fitting they should be
the last customers
before the place is kaput.

The sun snaps shut
like a casket lid over Flower Street.
By the open door,
a table is set for two.
Levin remains silent,
still holds a grudge,
jealous that Zablon outlived him
but more concerned with his hands
tied to the chair
with the *tzitzit* from his old *tallit*.

He sits wide-eyed, surprised,
slightly displeased,
even more thin skinned
than before,

but with broken-tile teeth
& a sense of Sabbath ease,
a calm easterly wind
that is laughter resounding.
Even when Zablon's head
begins to bounce to his chest,
heavy from prayer,
ready for sleep,
his *kappa* falling leaf-slow
into the hollow of his lap,
everything stills,
just for a minute
like in old western movies
to focus the audience
on something so easily missed
if the director had not made us
stop & see. Tonight,
Zablon seems close
to understanding this world.

***

The gray mop in the gray bucket
falls over, splashing gray water
on the gray stone floor.

The whole place smells
gray and smoky.
A chipped ceramic bowl,
filled with honey
rests in the middle
of a plate of apples,
sliced, skin-peeled,
just the way they like it.

In the sad kitchen,
the tea shrills.

Zablon brings two cups
boiling golden green tea.

Levin, with his jaw unhinged,
refuses to drink.

Zablon has not yet awakened.
Everything hurts. The dream

is a never-ending song.
The night worms its way in.

Interview with Z. S.

You once said you read poems the day your family "ran away". What were you reading?

Poetry? What do you know of poetry? Of pain? Of *my* people?

Oh well, Whitman, Ginsburg, Dickinson—

Bird calls. I spit on your songs. Sing to me a death cry, children throwing rocks & armed thugs who tear art from the wall, watch & laugh as two men swarm into the temple, take the five scrolls & depart. The others take my books. Look they left the calendar. Do you know why?

The Hebrew letters were too—

Letters? No. The dates are meaningless butterflies, beautiful perhaps but harmless.

What makes you sad?

Feh. You do not know what is important.

So what is important? Why are you here?

Why are any of us here? You bring your American zoo here, snap this, snap that. Write it down for more Americans to read. Then what? What happens next? You go on to the next story—

Poem.

Poem, story. What is the difference? You want to be less afraid.

Yes, I am afraid.

Ha! Yes, you are scared. Of course! This risk, coming here, it will show you extinction.

I see it in your eyes.

Tsk, tsk. No. Look. Look closer. You see a mirror.

Finding Yehud

Yak / 1

I take my Jewish muse
out for an evening stroll,
kiss my gold-chained *chai*
for luck the way my grandfather did
before he began his patrol,
tuck it deep into the secrets
of my chest hairs.

I exit the double-walled house,
turn down a street with no sign.
A jewelry store becomes a souvenir stand
becomes a series of floral shops.

I'm looking for answers
in a country seeded with questions.
The napkin in my hand is a map
with wavy lines & stick figures
from a cabbie in a ten-year-old Corolla.
I'm almost ready to turn back.

du / 2

Outside an Internet café,
the store owner sweeps
petals, twigs, cigs,
& head down, focused
on what tomorrow might bring.
He's not so different from you.

Inside, I buy a cup of tea
for an old man & he tells me
in perfect English
to go a few doors down, just past
the carpet dealer. I try not to look eager
to meet him.

se / 3

The delicious scent of baking bread
comes from a stranger's open window.

The white-washed building blends
with the others & I almost pass it.

The place ghosts the block—
more of a whisper than a haunt,

no chains to rattle here, still
I hesitate to enter.

Beneath the synagogue,
a yellow sign marks

his kabob restaurant. Inside,
above a faded menu

& a broken clock,
images of hunting

tape the wall. No smells
to welcome me in.

I sit at a Formica table
near a stack of boxes.

He bellies over with a dirty rag,
points to the door & says closed

in a language I can't identify.
I say *American*

as in loud,
as in lost.

I palm my heart, *here,*
Yehud. We're the same. Tell me—

how to find such strength,
how to know such faith?

chAr / 4

He holds out one hand,
releases a practiced smile,

points to the synagogue,
or perhaps higher,

says *Journalist or Jew,*
pay & we go tour.

Dusty & thirsty,
overheated,

I think about the time wasted,
the mistake being here.

He has no interest
in me. I'm not the first Jew

who wants to understand
his purpose.

I expected eyes full of apple-honey
to share prayers & feel a kin, find

the lost tribe.
Yet I see only *pul*-gray eyes

waiting & ready
to be paid.

The Last Act of an Unwritten Play

Yellow-white like mid-day sun, the stacked square pavers still stand, a half-built house or half-fallen. Many stones are cracked, open chunks or thin spread webs, nested with folded papers or patches of green weeds. Every day except Saturday, the old man appears, sits hunched,   backpressedtothe wall, familiar friends sharing a space, sharing secrets. He grips a carefully written prayer rolled like a cigarette, chants in a forgotten language. Wearing a small cap & his grandfather's shawl, he forgets the meaning of it but keeps the tradition. The horizon scalds with white light. A few students stop with change. Tourists tap their digital guidebooks, read about Kotel & Herod, the bulldozed Moroccan Quarter. A small footnote mentions the old man, not by name, just his song

Interview with Grandmother

"Because the smoke still drifted through your lives."
—Harvey Shapiro

Auschwitz was a hollow bowl of starvation. Everyone stole bread & cold soup from the dying. During her first winter, she took the treat of raw oatmeal & ate one flake after another, careful to lick each finger. This was before the nights of burning cosmos & dry dreams where she reached for water she could not hold, the sores lasting for months, blankets filled with cold, the memory of a butter sandwich, diarrhea days, broomstick bones & the deflated-balloon of flesh—her *Kaddish* was too much. She laid a hand on my shoulder so I couldn't leave. She did not stop, stating the event like late-night news: the digging, the clock of rails, fences everywhere, the throat of the loudspeaker, the mouth of night, the walking, the lines, more digging, the fear, the constant itch, those moth-filled skies, the ash, a pocketful of *kippah*

Sometime after This

the next last Jew
        will be born,
       after you read this,

with *matzah* colored skin
       & Talmudic
       eyes,
   with the breath
       of a lost language
       that speaks
            to salt & ash,

begins
    with *baruch*,
    beginning of a prayer,
        which most ignore

like the bearded veteran
    who holds a sign
    which could be a board
        from the ark
on the corner
   of Main
   & 10th.

For a few,
       it will feel familiar
       like the moment
          right before
   a sneeze
   & the bless
you, a fraction
of a second
       where you know
       what will come next,
         & then
   it is
   gone.

Glossary

Afghan Bread — This is also called *nan,* a soft, pocket-like bread, and it is considered the national bread of Afghanistan. It is oval shaped and baked in a tandoor oven. Black cumin is sprinkled on the bread for an added taste.

Aliyah — (Hebrew) the immigration to Israel, and it means "ascent".

Baruch — bless (The first word of the prayers that always begin 'Bless the God' or "*Baruch atah Adonai*".).

Bima — an elevated platform in synagogues where the Torah is read.

Chai — means living and consists of the Hebrew alphabet *chet* and *yod.* It is a spiritual number in Judaism and symbol of life; many Jews give gifts of money in multiples of 18 as a result

Diaynu — means "it will suffice" and often said as part of the Passover prayers and meal.

Drams — the currency of Armenia

Falooda — Afghan sundae topped with nuts

Gelt — Hanukah coins, either real or chocolate, given to children during the Jewish holiday.

Kippa — also known as a yarmulke that is worn mostly by Jewish men in order to cover their heads as a sign of respect for God.

Kugel — is a Jewish casserole served as a side dish during certain holidays and sometimes on Shabbat. It is usually made from noodles or potatoes with other ingredients mixed in.

Latkes — shallow-fried potato pancakes, topped with apple sauce or sour cream, and often served during Hanukah.

Magen David — Hebrew for "Star of David", a six pointed star that is a symbol in the Jewish faith.

Matzah Balls — dumplings made from matzah meal and often served during Passover in soup. It is interesting to note that the largest ever made at Noah's Ark Deli weighed 267 pounds and was 29.2 inches long.

Menorah — a nine-branched candelabrum that is part of Hanukah where each night another candle is lit to celebrate an ancient miracle. It is often made of some metal.

Mezuzah — religious decorative item placed on outer door frames of homes that contains a prayer within it.

Oghi — not associated with Jews but an Armenian vodka distilled from Mulberry fruit. Outside of Armenia the flavor is different and called *ouzo* in Greece or *raki* in Turkey.

Olim — (Hebrew) those who "make aliyah" are called an oleh (m. singular) or olah (f. singular) and the plural for both is olim.

pul — 1/100th of Afghani, the legal currency in Afghanistan.

Shalom — (Hebrew) meaning "peace, completeness, and welfare" but often used as a greeting and a parting as in hello and goodbye.

Shamash — It means "servant" and it is the ninth holder, usually the one in the center that is used to light the other candles for Hanukkah. The shamash must be offset on a higher or lower plane than the main eight candles.

Shofar — a ram's horn used to call in the New Year by making a loud horn-like sound.

Shul — a Hebrew word for temple or synagogue.

Simchat Torah — This is a religious service that is a celebration marking the conclusion of the finishing the annual cycle of reading the Torah and marks the starting over of reading the Torah. It occurs in mid-September to early October. In many synagogues, this is the only time of year on which the holy Torah scrolls are taken out of the ark at night, and when this happens, everyone leaves their seat to dance and sing.

Tallises — a prayer shawl worn over the outer clothes during the morning prayers.

Talmud — one of the main Judaic texts, referring to Jewish laws, customs and history.

yak, du, se, chAr — one, two, three, four: numbers in Eastern Persian or Dari, one of the two languages of Afghanistan.

yehud — this is Dari, one of the official languages of Afghanistan, for "The Jew", the nickname for Zablon Simintov.

Zhan Zhuang — means "standing like a tree" and is roughly pronounced "Jan Juang", or, in southern China, "Jam Jong". This posture is Tai Chi and considered to be the most powerful of all the postures, often used as a separate exercise to increase leg strength, concentration, deep breathing and chi flow.

About the Author

M. E. Silverman, editor of the *Blue Lyra Review*, moved in the wake of Katrina from New Orleans to Georgia. His chapbook, *The Breath before Birds Fly* (Emerging Literary Press, 2013), is available. His work has appeared in 70 journals including *Crab Orchard Review, December, Chicago Quarterly Review, The Los Angeles Review, Pacific Review, Many Mountains Moving, The Labletter, Naugatuck River Review, North Chicago Review, The Southern Poetry Anthology, Cloudbank, Veils, Halos and Shackles: International Poetry on the Abuse and Oppression of Women, Mizmor L'David Anthology: The Shoah,* and other journals and anthologies. M. E. Silverman was a finalist for the 2008 *New Letters* Poetry Award, the 2008 DeNovo Contest and the 2009 *Naugatuck River Review* Contest. He also co-edited an anthology called *Bloomsbury's Anthology of Contemporary Jewish American Poetry*. He has two more anthologies forthcoming: one on longish poems and one on the Holocaust. He lives with his wife, his daughter, and Marie, the unwanted cat who daily breaks into their house through the heating vents.

Glass Lyre Press

exceptional works to replenish the spirit

Glass Lyre Press is an independent literary publisher interested in technically accomplished, stylistically distinct, and original work. Glass Lyre seeks diverse writers that possess a dynamic aesthetic and an ability to emotionally and intellectually engage a wide audience of readers.

Glass Lyre's vision is to connect the world through language and art. We hope to expand the scope of poetry and short fiction for the general reader through exceptionally well-written books, which evoke emotion, provide insight, and resonate with the human spirit.

Poetry Collections
Poetry Chapbooks
Select Short & Flash Fiction
Anthologies

www.GlassLyrePress.com

www.ingramcontent.com/pod-product-compliance
Lightning Source LLC
Chambersburg PA
CBHW021157080526
44588CB00008B/385